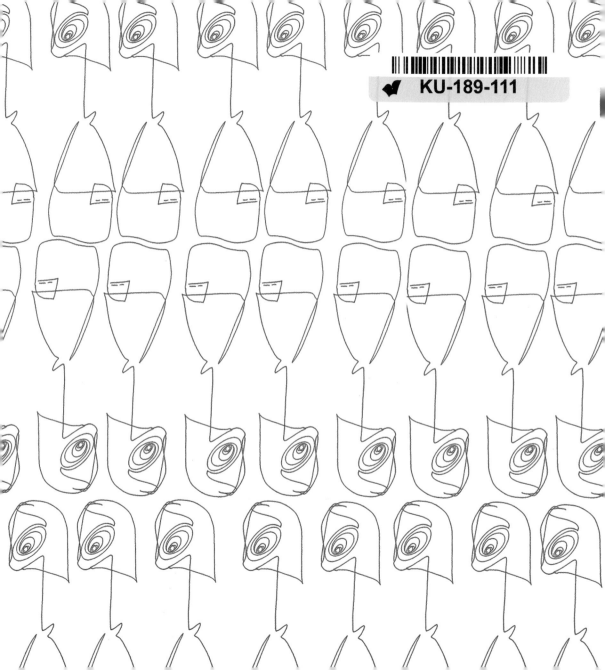

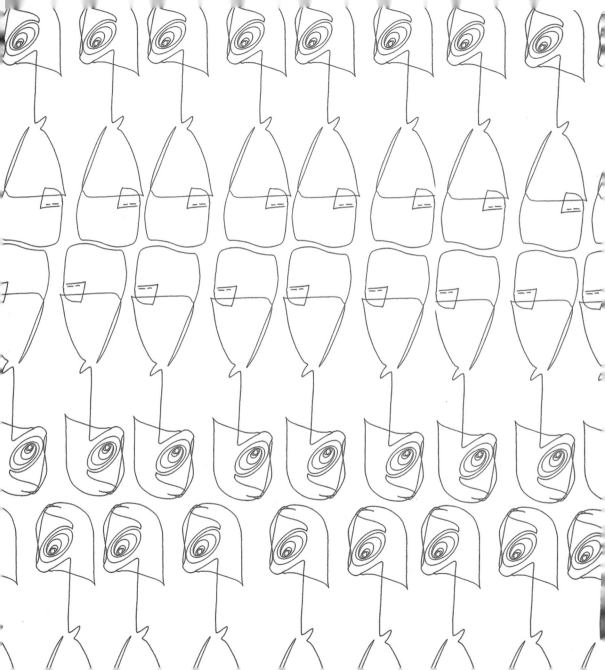

This Afternoon
and I

Sarah Roby

Templar Poetry

First Published 2013 by Templar Poetry

Fenelon House

Kingsbridge Terrace

58 Dale Road

Matlock

Derbyshire

DE4 3NB

www.templarpoetry.co.uk

ISBN 9781906285562

For permission to reprint or broadcast these poems write to Templar Poetry

A CIP catalogue record of this book is available from the British Library.

Typeset by Pliny

Cover Design Artwork by Jane Weir

Printed and bound in The European Union

For John and Jem

Acknowledgements

'H. Rider Haggard's Bare-Knuckle Wrestle with Time-on-his-Hands' was shortlisted for the Keats-Shelley Prize; 'Ritual' featured in *Poetry Review*.

Contents

H. Rider Haggard's Bare-Knuckle Wrestle with Time-on-his-Hands

AVeyMeyChristmasss. We find Rider Haggard resting on his royalties,
She just published, in 1921. You would recognise him in a snapshot
and insatiate as a self-pleasing crashing disappointment in bed.

His bookish eyes have shrunk to those of a mole unused to *brightlights!*
His upper lip has been sucked clean away in years of tentative, writerly
apprehension. He has totted his earnings in calligraphic ink *£Look!!!!*

AVeyMey. He has earned his place in the Ancient, Reckless and Independent
Order of Prevaricators: *This is to certify that H. Rider Haggard is entitled to lie
from the 1st day of January to the 31st day of December, he being a duly qualified Liar.*

It is signed the Secretary of State for his Infernal Majesty. (All swashbucklers
have gold pacts with the devil.) He has lied through mines and women,
women's mines and women's minds. He has lied through impossible loops

in impossible holes. Safe. Now he counts sales, acreage, days until the diary
cools to weather reports alone - dull to middling - and to much rabbit shooting,
where probability is high, risk low. And he does lie on a farm in Ditchingham,

looking up from where the earth is cold and the sky a colourless stratus,
and where the mine glitters to nauseous, changing nothing whatsoever.
He lies flat as a Norfolk native while the truth multiplies like...

African Queen

We are an odd couple, this afternoon and I.
One is prim through the dipping hours;
the other is sloughed in front of a matinée.

This afternoon is sharp as light and holier-than-cat;
its angles drawn to a missionary's chin that rests
its point on my shoulder. I shrug and smile

at its cartoon natives - the bright whiteness
and conspicuous hurry, the blood-sugar plunge -
and stare back into technicolour, when it was new.

We are bound together by a forwards escape
into evening and this afternoon is pragmatic,
technical and planning to use the very air:

What if we were to use our supply of oxygen canisters?
What if we filled them with the gelatine? If we brushed
against something at speed, surely we'd make…

I continue to dare leisure into the white waters
at four and past the bullets ticking five until
this afternoon makes me laugh with its impressions

of dark, its funny-mirror shadows that find us tall
and suddenly touching. We cloak dusk in thin innuendo:
Does this flower have a name? Well, if it doesn't, it sure is pretty.

In the dark, in this afternoon's legacy, things happen;
ideas come and bump up against one another.
We have swum home with a shanty, seizing the… *Torpedo!*

Levity III

It is late Sunday afternoon when we step inside Levity III,
leaving our shoes at the flapping door. 'This is a place
to relax,' a guide tells us, 'Rather like a hot air balloon.
Mind the little ones though, they're easy to lose.'

We begin in a green room, blown up and lit from behind,
and so close to yellow that our son has to check with us,
'It won't take off, will it?' From here, there is a choice
of tunnels, hollow as hands cupping a telescope in mime.

Further in, we find a maze of minarets and caves, turrets
and horns, blue and green, silver and purple. We find
a chamber, red and webbed, like inside the masked head
of a superhero thinking blood or love. Other visitors

collapse on soft walls that breathe a mother's earliest
rise and fall. I get a balled t-shirt pressed in the socket
of my palm where our son has found leverage to run,
a bouncy particle in this castle. He is soon in the company

of two old women who turn cartwheels in tandem.
'Come and join us,' they call, 'We're the loopy aunts.'
At this point, I am aware of you sighing, weary, as we push
on to a blue room that crowds our eyes to half irises.

Now our son is running, charging the many channels,
leaping against walls that return him in a rapid slide
to the ground until a guide, twitching, can no longer
resist and reprimands in a tone too soon for him.

The two aunts reappear and our son joins them
in swimming the floor. I see you blink, heavy-lidded,
effortful in patience, and so I call to a laughing version,
there only this morning, 'John!' You lean over,

bump your shoulder against mine, let a defence or two
fall, and smile. We return to our shoes, forced on
by dinner, bath time, a story, maybe some work,
leaving just before we are about to lift off.

The Present Participle

On Sunday we sit with spellings of present participles,
our heads still swept every which way by sleep.

Bound by the desk, I pull and my son pushes the loop
and queue of letters across the page in 17 words

for movement. Conditional I wonder: how should we move
– really move? On the page, our heads still tidal

or outside, on the scene, with its sometime patterns
of endorsement: *Well done, son.* He needs it;

needs his Sunday trees to climb. And I too need to be
outside but pointing at all the new emperors.

Later, much later, he will say she noticed too much
when a thick skin would have been warmer.

He drops the 'e' or doubles the consonant - *hoping, hopping* –
and joins us in handwriting: *I'm going now, Mum.*

I-Spy in the Home

I-spied outside on the blossom.
Flashes of red, flashes of black. Tick.

I-saw swung on the hang of June
bitten bloom, with my little eye. Tick.

I-catching spread as paper, drunk
on pollen, something beginning. Tick.

I-witness sudden fold, wings in
two, surrender. Tick, Oblivion, Tick.

I miss solid ground, walking out
wide open windows.Cross.Stitch.Kiss.

The Aurelian

Sometimes it's not enough to just watch a butterfly
shot like a paper aeroplane into one long, hot Sunday.
I want to net it, stop it, pin it, the old-fashioned way.

This isn't always easy but a sure swipe and a short spell
in a jar for it to sit thinking - like a good idea on
a chloroform cloud - can ready a butterfly for pinning.

I like to airlift its shape to the page so that it lies like
two open palms waiting to catch, although too often
the wings are already beginning to stiffen before they land.

I'll begin pinning with a line through the thorax —
to get to the meat of it. This might be short and delicate
for smaller moths or long and thick for the robust exotics.

Then follows the gentle lapping of forewing with hindwing,
forewing with hindwing, and the gradual pinning down
of each new idea for colour or marking. After a fortnight,

a butterfly can look completely dry whereas I prefer it
to sit like feathers on paper hinting at past flights. So
I may need to relax it a bit with, say, a jolt of hot water

again to the thorax. In the later stages, I'll label it,
tail to antennae, in the language of lepidoptera.
The last thing I like to do is frame it in a glass-topped box.

Fantasy

On head repeat:
a soldier, an arm lost
and running in the sun.
Where did pain and fantasy
first meet?

On bone heels,
sat too cross-legged
on the soles of my feet;
the early, slow location
of hard dreams.

                *

On a loop:
Billie Holliday in blue
and the moon raining
cool, white quavers
'til I am duped

by tragedy;
how I'd go through
teal, indigo, near-black experience
just to come close
to that soul edge.

Ongoing:
a slow, Bovary afternoon
to milk fictions dry, to rub
pipedreams, all the time
knowing

that for all
the of-the-moment,
at-the-circus, audacious possibility
of the thought bubble,
we stall.

       *

On paper:
Rossetti's fetish·for low-slung fruit
and dwarves; mine for men-in-uniform
and melancholia;
I am ever

reaching, slow
to realise how a history of hunching,
hair dripped, over white paper
will mean each new idea
begins *Within the willow.*

Ritual

Secular living still needs ritual
 - the gathering of us through thicks and thins,
people-deep around a new arrival
or the touch – just – of hands in grieving.
Patterns like these can soothe and form,
from templates pressed into the air,
a horse-shoe, love-heart or key-to-the-door
that make the invisible almost there.

And each one with its quirk of accuracy
is like a morning climb up the stairs
taking half a cup of tea exactly
in a gesture of some red ruby years;
or the faithful precision of a weekly row,
a reminder that we matter, here, now.

Ritual II

Secular living still needs ritual
and so we make our own from white paper,
a square, exact, smoothed in a valley fold,
scored with a deep crevice down the centre.
Two corners then drawn in one arrow head,
arched back and flat and blunted into half
until, over a mountain fold, wings spread
in a vapourless trail, sure as a dart.

Although we do not always make a plane,
some days the regular bend, tuck and crease
give us a boat, fish, a Japanese crane,
unable to lift from the room with ease.
One time we fold ourselves a windmill,
tall and waving, even when the breeze stills.

Protest Song

I saw PJ Harvey, Song Correspondent, on the news last night.
The rock and pop of the day's events in Iraq shot from the lipline.

Jaunty like the hetting up of my mother-in-law by a condition she's
read about that you don't know you've got. She called the ambulance.

I am struck by PJ Harvey, unused to the jutting of current truth
from the real-time relations of voice and guitar, and laugh at how

frontline emergency services must have reacted to complaints of
an imperceptible heart attack. My mother-in-law is put on a treadmill

and given a heart monitor. I listen to PJ's unison with an Iraqi woman
singing in Kurdish and her rage against the same mistake in the same place.

I hold a slim V of forefinger and middle finger to my wrist to feel
the beat of a protest song and find that my pulse remains the same.

How we grieve now

i.m. Michael Jackson

I am sick the mornings across August as the autopsy
on the front pages cuts deeper. My palate shifts,
sense of smell sharpens and I can no longer stomach
the taste of red in the tabloids. I carry with me all that might
become iconic: the pink shell of a dancer, kicking, the face
of a Caucasian male slipping into place and a white hand
beckoning to Neverland until, abrupt at twelve weeks,
the ultrasound returns a black-and-white photo without pulse.
Dead already, for some time and none of us knew.

Now thoughts of a baby, dangled, and later, of small children,
recede. In the papers, they stoop lower for possible causes
or details of paternity whilst I lean over – in agony now –
and scoop from the u-bend three solid centimetres,
ten weeks young. They become hard when they've been
up there a while. We start to try and lose what was never ours,
with bloody memorabilia, for one who never actually lived
but remained a boy prince. For this is how we grieve now.

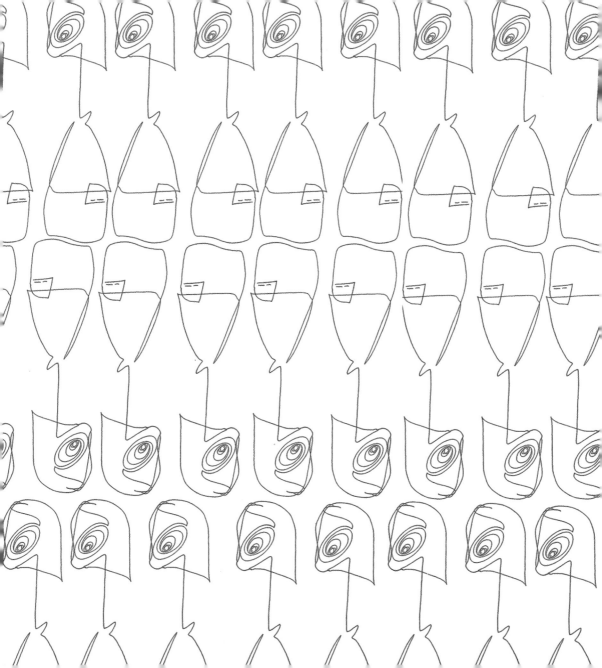

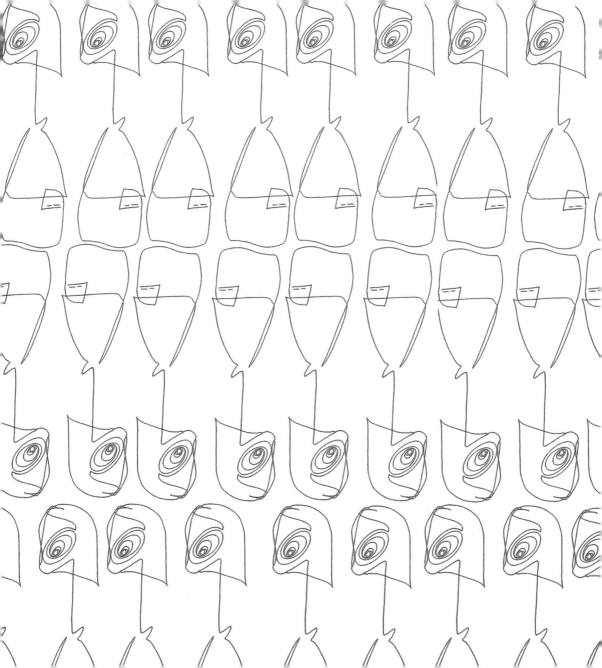